Investing For Beginners

How to Save, Invest and Grow Your Wealth Through the Stock Market, Real Estate, Index Funds, Precious Metals, and More

Joel Jacobs

Table of Contents

Introduction

Does one need to be a financial expert to trade and invest? Absolutely not. One needs to learn the basics of the financial market and then learn what works for them and what does not. Are you someone who wants short-term investments with huge risks but even higher payouts? Or are you someone who would rather make long-term investments to retire comfortably? Would you rather actively have control over your assets or have a professional handle them at a cost? Investing has a lot of subsets and strategies that can be molded to suit the individual.

Investments do incur risks; however, those risks can be minimized with the right trading tools and proper help. Investors know that they will incur losses, which is why they ensure that their generated revenues surpass those losses. Making smart financial investments can be profitable both in the short and the long run. There is no perfect time to start investing, so anyone interested in investing can begin trading anytime. Financial securities like stocks and shares have many variations that can benefit anyone depending on their financial standing and investment goals. Also, stocks and shares are not the only options when it comes to investing in the market. There are bonds, mutual funds, precious metals, and even real estate that one could invest in to generate revenues. In addition, many trading strategies exist for each of the financial securities, meaning there is an investment option for everyone.

So, want to tap into the world of investing but have no idea where to start? It might sound obvious, but in order to fully comprehend how investments work, we need to start at the very beginning and give definitions to all the terms that are going to be used persistently in this book. Learning the basics allows for a better understanding of the more complex notions of investing. It permits you, a future investor, to be fully comfortable with every aspect of the trade.

Chapter 1: Investment Basics for Beginners

What Is the Stock Market?

The stock market is a cluster of exchanges and markets that participate in the buying, selling, and trading of public and private company investment securities. Investment securities are tradable financials such as stocks, equities, and debt used to raise capital in both public and private markets with the purpose of retaining them for investment. These shares are almost always from public companies because private companies do not exchange their shares on the public stock market. Keep in mind that while private companies are not publicly traded, they still have shares that are kept and traded internally for their selective group of shareholders, such as employees. Let us return to the stock market. A country can have multiple stock exchange venues that follow the same regulations set in place by formal business institutions. In everyday dialogue, the terms stock market and stock exchange are often used interchangeably. However, a stock market is a collection of stock exchanges. For clarification, any market participating in the exchange of stocks and other financial securities is considered a stock market. In comparison, a stock exchange is the place where such trades are happening. For example, someone claiming they trade on the stock market means that they participate in purchasing and selling shares through one or more stock exchanges that the stock market encompasses. Some of the most popular American stock exchanges include NASDAQ and the New York Stock Exchange, which make up part of the American stock market.

To fully understand the purpose of the stock market, imagine that you are window shopping for a pair of jeans. Thankfully, the area that you live in is packed with denim vendors eager for your money. They will compete with each other to offer their consumers the best price for their product. Because of this, you are offered a fair price and are able to peruse the options before making your choice. However, your friend Ben lives in a smaller town with only one denim vendor and is forced to purchase from that one vendor when he needs jeans. Similarly, the stock market is the meeting place of various options when it comes to shares and stocks. This abundance of financial securities ensures fair pricing, healthy competition, and trading security in a secure and controlled environment. With the use of modern-day technology, the stock market operates electronically, allowing for zero to low operational risk.

There are various markets within the stock market that have different specializing characteristics, despite an occasional overlap in functionality. Two subcategories of stock markets include the equity market and the share market.

What Is the Equity Market?

As part of the stock market, the equity market refers to the buying and selling of ownership shares of public companies through the stock exchange. Therefore, the equity market does not deal with the exchanging of privately traded stocks. Both terms are synonymous in investing because purchasing a share of stock constitutes an equity interest in a company. Someone buying a stake in a company has the expectation to benefit from their investment, either through the price of the stock increasing or receiving a share of the profits. Just like stock markets, equity markets are an all-encompassing term for all global stock exchanges that pair public stock buyers with public stock sellers. The biggest examples of equity markets include the New York Stock Exchange, Hong Kong Exchanges, and Euronet Europe. The equity market is typically the stock market that people are the most familiar with, and at its core, it follows a free-market economic system. Public companies turn a profit by participating in the equity market and allowing investors to purchase ownership of the said company through shares. The number of shares an investor possesses determines the percentage of company ownership they have.

However, while the stock market deals with both public and private company stocks, the equity market focuses on public company stocks. Stocks are offered by buyers at prices and then sellers will bid for their specific prices, and when the two match, a sale happens. The price of an asset in the marketplace or its value determined by the investment community is referred to as the market value. This is easy to determine for exchange-traded securities like stocks. These stocks are considered liquid since they are easily bought, sold and traded, which influences their market value. For example, if there are a high number of investments in a company then the price of their stock will rise. On the other hand, an increase in investors selling their stocks of a company will decrease the value of their stocks.

What Is the Share Market?

As previously discussed, the share market is a subset of the stock market that handles the purchasing and selling of shares, which represent a unit of ownership of whichever company the share comes from. The purchasing of shares permits companies to maintain their upkeep and allows investors to trade shares to profit. Since the exchange of shares also happens in an equity market, it is easy to confuse the two markets and their similarities. A difference between the two is that a shareholder, or someone investing in company shares, owns the shares of one specific company. In contrast, an equity stockholder is someone who buys stock in any company. Both are very similar but found in different categories of the stock market.

What Is the Over-the-Counter Market?

Independent stock exchanges are called over-the-counter (OTC) markets, and just like their physical stock exchange counterparts, they exist all over the globe. These are decentralized markets in which the participants can directly trade stocks, currencies, and more without the need for a broker. They do not have a physical location; instead, all exchanges are performed electronically or over the phone. These are very different from auction-based market systems, where buyers and sellers both simultaneously compete in bidding and offering of stocks. The price of an exchanged stock through this system represents the lowest rate a seller is willing to sell and the highest rate a buyer is willing to spend. This kind of market has two types of clientele: a broker trading with their clients, including corporations and institutions, is called a "customer market," while two traders exchanging with each other are referred to as an "interdealer" market.

In over-the-counter markets, however, dealers participate in shaping the market by creating their own prices to buy and sell a security or another financial product. Due to there being fewer regulations in OTC markets than physical stock markets, exchanges can occur without anyone else knowing much about the trade, including the pricing of the transaction. Because of this, over-the-counter markets are less transparent and have liquidity due to the occasional lack of both buyers and sellers. The dependency on the market influencing dealers can make it troublesome to buy and sell stocks in the future.

What Are Primary and Secondary Markets?

Markets fall into one of two divisions: primary and secondary markets. In the primary market is the creation of new financial securities, including bills and stocks for companies trading for the first time, usually at a pre-determined or arranged price. This market issues and sells new stocks and bonds to the public. A popular example of such is an initial public offering or IPO. During an initial public offering, a business transpires between the purchasing investor and the financing bank in charge of underwriting the IPO. An important thing to understand is that securities created by the primary market are purchased straight from an issuer. Governments and companies will both use this market by issuing new securities in order to expand business operations and to cover research and development expenses. They achieve this because the majority of the funding earned goes to the issuer of the securities-in this case, the companies and governments. Financing that does not go to an issuer can go to an investment bank that intervenes and regulates the initial pricing of securities, receiving a portion of the funding for facilitating sales. Trading on the primary market is also beneficial for investors who will commonly pay less on securities compared to the secondary market.

While the primary market handles stocks when they are first issued to the public, the secondary market encompasses the purchasing and selling of securities that investors already own. In this way, investors trade with each other instead of trading with the financial security issuing entity. Since there are many independent but interconnected trades, the secondary market acts as an equalizer, driving the price of securities towards their actual valued price. When most people think of investing and the stock market, they are thinking of the secondary market. The most commonly traded securities in the secondary market are stocks; however, they are definitely not the only financial asset traded on this market. Individual investors, corporations, and investment banks can purchase and trade bonds and mutual funds, such as real estate mortgages, on the secondary market. All these trades benefit the selling investor who receives all the proceeds from their sales instead of the company issuing the stock or the bank underwriting the IPO.

Secondary market transactions are called this because they are one step removed from the original securities created in the primary market. For instance, a financial institution creating mortgage security by writing mortgages for consumers would be the primary market. Then, the bank would sell such securities to real estate corporations and associations on the secondary market.

Who Are Brokers?

Brokers are firms or individuals who act as intermediaries between investors and the exchange of securities. They are essential because securities exchanges only approve of orders and trades between individuals and firms already participating in that exchange. Therefore, individual investors and traders require the services of exchange members, or brokers. These financial intermediaries are compensated for their service through administrative fees, commissions, or getting paid directly from the trade itself. Brokers can also provide potential investors with financial guidance by offering their market intelligence, investment plans, and client-tailored market research.

In investing, there are two types of brokers: discount brokers and full-service brokers. The former administers exchanges on their client's behalf without typically providing financial advice or insight. At the same time, the latter includes tailored financial investment solutions and advice in addition to their exchange service. Due to the growth of online stock exchanges, the number of discount brokers has increased immensely. They are great for self-directed investors who do not require any investment advice or research services. Discount brokers are often paid in fees rather than a commission. They keep their prices cheap due to the volume of trading they execute and their lower administrative costs compared to brokers working on non-online platforms.

In comparison, full-service brokers offer a variety of services ranging from market research to retirement planning, in addition to their investment products. Because of all of this, these brokers charge potential investors far more in commission for their services. Full-service brokers are then compensated through a brokerage firm based on both trading volume and investment product sales. Recently, instead of a commission payment system, some full-service brokers offer investment products and services for a set fee; this can include products like managing clients' investment accounts.

Despite the terms "broker" and "trader" being used synonymously in everyday conversation, there is a notable distinction between the two. A trader is someone who trades and buys stocks on behalf of a portfolio manager, while a broker is a licensed financial sales agent. There are many similarities between the two, such as they both sell and trade securities for their clientele, who can either be individuals or corporations. However, the main difference is that the broker has direct contact with their clients while the trader does not.

What Is a Demat Account?

A dematerialized account, or Demat account for short, provides the convenience of maintaining financial securities in an electronic format. It holds all of an individual's investments, including shares, exchange-traded funds, and bonds, in one place. Thus, investors participating in online trading with a Demat account benefit from electronic security, convenience, and cost-effectiveness. Dematerialization in this sense is the process of converting traditional physical share certificates into electronic forms, offering a modernized, easy-to-maintain format for investors to see all their holdings at any time and anywhere in the world. Due to their online formatting, Demat accounts help reduce costs and risks associated with physical certificates, and paperwork. They also offer users the ease of seeing all their investments in one place quickly, without the need for a paper trail.

Think of Demat accounts like a bank account. Just like a bank account, a dematerialized account holds the account holder's securities in electronic form instead of a physical form and keeps track of credits and debits of their financial securities.

Why Do Shares Fluctuate?

The price of shares changes every day by market forces, following the concept of supply-demand economics. This means that if the demand for shares surpasses the supply of current shares, then the price increases to match the demand. This happens because many buyers want the same limited shares, therefore driving up the price as only those with the capital can purchase them. The opposite also applies; if the supply of shares surpasses the demand, the price will drop to entice people to buy the supply surplus. This is the reason for the daily fluctuations in shares. The supply and demand of shares globally are determined by individual corporations and how financially well they do. In addition, there are other external and internal variables that can fluctuate the pricing of shares, depending on their effect on the market. These price fluctuations are seen as market risk and are beyond the investors' control.

What Are Dividends?

Publicly-listed companies can reward investors who put money into their venture in the form of dividends. A dividend gets distributed out of a company's earnings to a select group of its shareholders, who are determined by the company's board of directors. These income distributions are typically cash, but they can also be in the form of additional stock in the company. Dividend payouts are commonly accompanied by a proportional increase in the company's stock price. Although dividends come out of a company's profits, they can still be paid out if profits are not made. The reason for this is to maintain a public image for current investors and potential new ones.

The board of directors can decide both the number of payout rates and the frequency of dividend payouts. Quarterly payouts are common; however, they can also be paid out monthly or yearly. Through scheduled or individual dividend payouts, companies might issue non-recurring special dividends for investors as a bonus reward. An example of such a special dividend is Microsoft, who, due to strong business performance and an increased financial outlook, issued a $3 per share in 2004 while the average at the time was $0.08 to $0.16 per share.

Dividends create a dialogue of trust between investors and companies, following the concept of "I scratch your back, you scratch mine." Companies will reward investors in hopes of more investments leading to future higher dividend payouts. These company payouts also offer insight into a companies' financial situation and can be a way to reassure shareholders about the future of the company. Companies with long, robust dividend payout records are often more trusted than the alternative. A reduction or complete elimination of a dividend payout could indicate to investors that the company is in trouble; it can also mean that the board of directors decided that the profits were better used for internal investment. Perhaps investing that financial surplus into a new product or service could triple profits in the future, and this was deemed as more important.

The best dividend payers are often larger, established companies in the market with predictable profits. They issue regular dividends to maximize shareholder wealth and build a rapport of trust with their investors. The companies often work in healthcare, the oil industry, banks, utilities, and basic materials. Start-ups and companies known for high growth, like the technology industry, may not offer dividends to their investors. These early-stage companies may incur high costs and losses that could have been used for the company. These companies might not have enough profit to supply dividends but still make enough money to sustain themselves. Companies might also not pay out dividends in order to invest their profits back into the business, especially during the process of expansion or moments of high growth.

What Types of Investors Are There?

In stock exchanges, there are two main types of investors: short-term and long-term investors. Short-term investors are traders who will buy and sell shares daily or weekly in order to profit on the face value price fluctuations of their shares. This kind of investor can also hold their shares for longer amounts of time but will commonly sell their shares when the price is high. At the same time, they buy shares when stock prices are lower than usual or when a market price increase is upcoming. On the other hand, long-term investors will buy stocks in bulk and invest over a long period of time. These types of investors do not worry about the face value growth of the shares. Instead, they are concerned with the dividend payouts from their company investments.

In more depth, short-term investors hold their financial securities for less than a year, typically for a couple of months, and use their liquidity and active trading strategies to generate revenues. These forms of investment include but are not limited to short-term bonds, stocks, ETFs, and more. Short-term investors count on the volatility of their investments. The fluctuations in price allow for these traders to profit off a financial asset in a certain amount of time. Despite the relatively small price movements of these assets in the market, these securities usually have high liquidity, ensuring that investors can sell them fairly quickly. Traders in this category can trade multiple securities with smaller price fluctuations to make smaller, more consistent gains. They can also act on the high volatility of certain assets and attempt to capitalize on sudden, more drastic price movements. An example of this is an investor selling their stocks after they have experienced appreciation in price, therefore earning in profits the difference between the sold price and the initial purchased price. Short-term investments are usually a form of active investing and carry a higher risk of losing capital since the market can fluctuate in any direction. One bad investing decision can cost traders a lot of money. Therefore, a lot of research, market knowledge, and confidence are needed to comfortably trade securities in the short term.

Long-term investors, on the other hand, hold the majority of their assets for up to a couple of years. These long-term investments are commonplace in financial portfolios with a specific investing strategy tailored for the investor. These investments include mutual funds, long-term savings accounts, and bonds. Although almost any investment can become a long-term one, securities with slow but steady value appreciations are favored. Illiquid investments, or securities that cannot be quickly transferred into cash, are also common long-term investments. Real estate is a popular long-term investment, where investors will buy properties and let them naturally appreciate in value. Other than this, long-term investments make for good college funds and retirement accounts because these portfolios count on long-term value growth and limited trading and transactions. These longer investments are considered a form of passive investing since less oversight and management is needed.

These two types contain many subsets and hybrids of the two investment ideologies, which can be tailored to individual financial circumstances and investment goals. This will be explored more in-depth in future chapters.

What Are Sectors?

Industries and sectors are synonymous terms that define any given economy in a market. Companies get assigned an industry based on their primary line of business, and their associations with similar industries are aggregated into a major sector. Therefore, sectors are huge generic categories of about a dozen economic industries , with each industry followed by sub-industries.

The majority of economies have four sectors, which in turn are cut into sub-sectors. The first of these sectors is the primary sector, which consists of the extraction of earth's natural products. Industries in this sector are agriculture, mining, and forestry. The secondary sector involves manufacturing and the processing of the primary sector's products into new goods. The tertiary sector provides services for products such as entertainment firms, retailers, and financial institutions. The last sector, titled the quaternary sector, includes companies working with intellectual pursuits, such as educational organizations.

Sectors allow investors to invest their money in classified business industries such as healthcare, technology, and telecommunications. Each and every sector has its own characteristics and associated risks that attract investors. Because of this, many economic analysts will specialize in one sector, with large companies having many advisors per sector. This also creates the notion of sector investing, where one may only invest in one sector they deem beneficial for them. The gas and oil industry is a popular sector that attracts many specialized investments. Stocks will often trend alongside their respective sector, meaning if a whole sector is having a rough year, chances are any stocks associated with that sector will fall. Therefore, having an understanding of the market will allow investors to estimate the rise and fall of a particular stock from whichever sector, based on the sector's overall performance.

Chapter 2: Investment in Stocks and Options

Now with the basics of investing and financial securities defined, we are ready to delve into the actual art of investing in stocks and options. First, we must categorize the different types of trading that can occur before further explaining the various forms of stocks and options in the financial investment world. These trading strategies all have their pros and cons. Each investor needs to determine which strategy works for them based on their initial capital and investment goals.

As a refresher, stocks are tiny portions of a public company that anyone can buy, or in the case of private companies, only internal shareholders can buy. An investor buying a stock in a company is investing money into a company and hoping that that stock will increase in value in the future, which is based on the company's financial well-being in question. Since the prices of stocks change daily, they are considered volatile. Thus, it is smart to buy stocks in different industries to have a diverse investment portfolio. A diverse portfolio will ensure that the investor has other investments to bounce back on even if one sector falls. Stocks are purchased either at physical locations such as an auction-based stock exchange like the New York Stock Exchange or through an online platform like NASDAQ.

The benefits of trading in stocks long-term are dividends, those regular company payouts to shareholders which depend on the company's current financial situation. For long-term stock investors, picking a larger company with a history of high regular dividend payouts and limited debt is key. Despite short-term stock traders forgoing dividends, they can still profit by buying stocks at low prices and selling them when their value increases. Since stocks fluctuate daily, this can be a quick way to make money.

As aforementioned, stock prices fluctuate easily, and their volatile nature can make them a risky investment. While one stock buyer is hoping that their purchased stocks will increase in value, another stock seller is anticipating for them to crash. With these changes happening so quickly, it can be difficult to know when to buy and sell. It is all about finding the investment technique that works for you based on your characteristics. Stock trading is fast and requires lots of time spent watching the market; however, it allows for quick profit if done right. The rapid pace of trading is also why a diverse financial portfolio is key when participating in the stock exchange. Investing in different sectors and having various kinds of investments spreads out the possibility of risk and allows you to maximize profit. Never put all your eggs in one basket.

Strategies of Trading in Stocks and Options

There are different styles of trading depending on the investor's goals and how quickly the investor can make a profit. There are long-term and short-term styles that can be used in conjunction with each other while other strategies oppose each other. It all depends on the investor's trading style and their aspired investment goals. All forms of trading can be categorized into two styles of investing: active and passive.

Active investing is a hands-on approach that requires someone to act as portfolio manager, whether they are hired or the investor themself. The goal of active investing is to take advantage of short-term price fluctuations to beat the stock market's average returns. This requires a deeper understanding of the market and the variables that affect the value of all securities. Most portfolio managers have a team of employees who use both quantitative and qualitative factors to make educated assumptions of market price changes to know when to buy and sell shares. This requires not only a vast knowledge of investing but also confidence in those trading decisions. A good portfolio manager must be more right than wrong about price fluctuations and good investments.

Passive investing is a long-term style of investing and is more cost-effective since the number of trades and transactions is limited. Passive investors cannot get swayed by market sentiment, fluctuations, and the temptation to anticipate the market's next move. This style of investing requires a buy-and-hold mentality just to allow the securities to run their course in order to benefit in the long term. Index Funds are good examples of passive investment as they are many tiny pieces of shares that participate in the overall uptrend of the market. This way, investors earn their returns over a long time, keeping their eye on the prize ahead and not caving into short-term shortcomings and setbacks.

A combination of both styles for short-term and long-term returns is favorable for any investor. Using a passive investment like a Mutual Fund to secure retirement income while actively day-trading shares for bigger short-term returns is an example of this.

Trend Trading

Trend Trading is a style of trading that involves following the market trends of industries and stocks to make investments. When the price of a stock fluctuates upwards or downwards, that is referred to as a trend. Trend trading analyzes the market for trends and uses that to take advantage of either uptrends or downtrends. Stocks that are on an uptrend mean that their value increases, with higher swing lows and higher swing highs. In contrast, value decreasing stocks on a downtrend experience lower swing highs and lower swing lows. Swing lows are when the lows of stock are lower than the surrounding stock prices at any given time. Swing highs are the opposite of a swing low, meaning the stock price is higher than other high stocks in that given time. Swing highs are usually the peak of a stock's value and are followed by a decline. This form of trading is great for investing beginners due to the ease of its application.

Investors who are trend trading will use these market trends to enter either a long position or a short position. Joining a long position refers to when an investor buys stocks with the assumption that they will rise in value in order to sell them at a profit in the future. This strategy is considered a long-term investment as one must wait for that uptrend. Historically, the stock market usually appreciates over time; however, that does not mean that those assumptions are always right and that a market crash is impossible. A global pandemic, anyone?

The opposite of a long position is a short position, which is when an investor sells their stock at its current price with the intention to rebuy it at a lower price after a downtrend. Short position trend trading is shorter term but riskier since there is more room for failure than there is for success. This is because investors in this position rely on a stock decreasing and their profits are based on how close to zero the value of the stock is. As mentioned before, the stock market is more likely to appreciate in value rather than depreciate. In short position trading, there are two types of short positioning: naked short and covered short. The former involves trading stocks that one does not own, while the latter borrows shares through a stock loan department to sell.

Naked shorting is a controversial topic since it is illegal in the United States, despite it still happening through regulation loopholes. Naked shorting is the act of short-selling shares that one does not own or have not been proven to exist. This has an impact on the liquidity of financial security in the marketplace. It allows investors to participate in a non-available stock exchange. If other investors also take part, it increases the liquidity and demand of a share that investors cannot obtain.

Contrarian Trading

Contrarian Trading is an eponymous investment style that involves investors intentionally going against market trends by selling stocks when most are buying and vice versa to turn profits. These types of investors argue that investors who follow trends are often too late for the market movement to be beneficial. Meaning, if the majority of people are assuming that the market will continue to uptrend, then the market is most likely already at its peak. The same works in reverse-if a downturn is predicted, that means the shares have already sold out and that the market can only start going upwards from here. Contrarian trading is built around the notion of market herd mentality that can fluctuate the market trends. While most people are following trends, contrarian investors are using other investors' pessimism to buy stocks that are deemed invaluable or sell stocks that everyone is buying in hopes of an uptrend.

This way of investing is more long-term because most of these investors buy undervalued stocks with the intention to sell once the value rebounds. This strategy does lead to profits when those undervalued stocks start to rise; however, it is a possibility that the stock will never recover. Because they do not follow trends, these investors can miss out big when the market trends are correct.

Candlestick Trading

Candlestick charts are used to show the link between price and the supply-demand influenced by the emotion of traders. Having originated from Japan in the 1700s when analyzing the rice market, candlestick charts use different colors to represent the size of price moves. Different colors are used to show which emotion is being displayed and its impact on price movements. These charts help traders determine possible price fluctuations based on past market patterns. A daily candlestick chart shows the four price points, which are open, close, high, and low.

Price Action Trading

Price Action Trading involves reading the current market based on historical data and price movements to make a subjective decision of whether or not to buy, sell or trade securities. Traders of this style will use technical analysis tools such as trend lines, financial charts, and high/low swings to create their unique strategy for trading. This requires an in-depth understanding of the market and comfort with data analytics.

Since this form of trading is based on the investor's subjectivity, no two traders will react the same way to price fluctuations, with one buying securities when another would sell. These subjective decisions are assisted by market research and data, but every trader has their own price point limitations, behavioral patterns, and interpretations of the market. One trader might use an upward trend, enter a long position and buy securities on the assumption that the security will continue to increase. Another can interpret an upward trend with an upcoming decline, enter a short position, and sell their securities while the price value is high.

The market can be unpredictable, and there is no sure-fire way to guess the future of price value. Price action trading is good for short- to medium-term investments and profit trades rather than long-term investments. Traders must use subjective thinking and data analytic tools to identify potentially profitable trade opportunities. It also has a lot of support in the investing industry.

Price action trading offers flexibility and independence to traders who understand the market and have access to market data. In addition to the ease of exchanging securities through trading software, this trading style allows investors to feel like they are in control of their investments and make the decisions that could make or break their investment portfolio.

News Trading

As aforementioned, the stock market usually trends upwards; however, crashes and other downfalls can destroy an investor's financial portfolio. Therefore, trading news about the market should be an integral part of any investor. A day trader should stay abreast of trading news and do so multiple times during an exchange session, while long-term investors need to follow trade news less frequently.

Most market trading news is scheduled, and these include quarterly economic reports and corporations' economic updates. These news updates can positively affect one sector while negatively affecting another, which is another reason why it is imperative to diversify one's portfolio to cushion one's losses with other securities. However, trading news does foster a herd investment mentality. Therefore if an investor is subjectively confident in their investment securities, they will stick to them. It is very contrarian, however, it has been stated that the market crowd sentiment is not always right.

Trading news is classified into two categories: recurring and one-time. Recurring news is scheduled news releases that fluctuate the market, and these refer to business' quarterly earning reports, bank interest rate announcements, and economic data releases. One-time news is unexpected events that affect the market; usually, these events are more bad than good. These events can include but are not limited to terrorist attacks, pandemics, and bankruptcy from corporations and countries. Market news can affect a specific stock, an industry or sector, or the whole market.

As an investor, trading news is a must in order to know when, where, and which sector to invest in. Keeping in mind important dates for corporations that you participate in is important to track fluctuations in the market. Have a strategy both for good trading news and bad; always know your exit route in case of investing emergencies. Avoid rash decisions by seeing the big picture of the market. An immediate fall in the agriculture industry due to a faulty tractor contract might mean new lower swing lows that could see an uptrend in the future. Every investor has their own maximum risk levels; what is yours? It is easy to get swayed by the market crowd sentiment. However, sometimes investors must know when to use the news to their advantage and when to ignore it. Investors in long-term positions have more freedom in ignoring news that will not affect their long position investments. The bottom line is that trading news is paramount in upkeeping one's portfolio and taking advantage of the market to boost investments and profits.

Algorithm Trading

Algorithm Trading, or automatic trading, uses online investment software that follows a determined set of rules or an algorithm to accomplish the trade of securities. The algorithm will perform trades based on rules set by the investor that include time, price, quantity, or anything else that can be input mathematically. This form of trading can generate a larger number of trades and at a greater speed than a human investor. It also makes trading more systematic by removing the market impact of human emotion from the equation as well as rendering the market more liquid.

Using a computer program to facilitate trades eliminates the need for the investor to manually keep track of market fluctuations and live security pricing. The algorithm set in place by the investor will automatically buy and sell securities whenever the trader's criteria are met. Trades through this system are executed instantly at the best selling price through the investment software and are timed to avoid changes in pricing. This automated investment strategy reduces manual human error and removes emotional trading that can be costly. Historical financial data and real-time data through the software can also help to validate trading strategies.

Traders also use automatic trading in different investment strategies to generate profits. Adopting market trends is a popular way to invest through this system. Using historical data to view trends, one can set up an algorithm to buy and sell when the securities are at their respective highs and lows. Also, since trades on this software are instant, investors use this platform to purchase low-priced securities in one market to resell them simultaneously in another market for a higher price. These almost risk-free profitable trades are called arbitrage opportunities and just require an implemented algorithm to notice the use of price differentials to place orders.

Fundamental Trading

Fundamental trading refers to a strategy where traders will focus on market or company-specific events to determine when to buy stocks and who to buy them from. This method is associated with long-term buy-and-hold strategies rather than short-term daily traders. Buy-and-hold refers to buying stocks and holding onto them regardless of market fluctuations in the hopes of a substantially profitable long-term return.

Fundamentalists make their trades based on fundamentalist analysis, which includes corporation economic releases. These releases are anticipated, actual or historical financial reports, company acquisitions, and reorganizations in addition to stock splits. These traders use this quantitative data to search for investment opportunities; however, with millions of people also investing, it can be hard to acquire any information or data that someone else does not already have. Despite this, there is a usual boost in trades after these earning reports, creating a short-term investing opportunity.

Stock Splits are also important in fundamental trading. For example, a company takes their $40 stock and splits it 2 for 1. There is now double the number of stocks on the market selling for $20. This stock split doesn't change the company's capital on the market, but more people are willing to buy a $20 stock compared to a $40 stock. Using stock splits and historical data, an investor can identify the four phases of stock split appreciation and depreciation. In the pre-split, the value of the stock will typically increase while decreasing in the post-split. Using this information, short-term split stock traders can generate profit multiple times in one day with the same stock.

Another part of fundamentalist analysis is acquisitions and corporate takeovers. These acquisitions follow the same market trend as stock splits. Oftentimes they have an uptrend during the takeover speculation phase of the acquisition announcement followed by an immediate downtrend afterward. Fundamentalist traders use these trends, historical data, and investment analysis to make subjective, fair decisions when it comes to trading.

Sentimental Trading

Sentimental trading is the act of trading securities based on the sentiment of the overall market and could be classified as the opposite of contrarian trading. The market sentiment is the majority consensus to the overall state of a stock or the market. Two terms come into play when referring to sentiments of the market: bullish and bearish. A bullish investor or a bull is one who believes that security prices will go up. This term can also describe the market as a whole; if the market sentiment is that prices will increase, then the market sentiment is bullish. Bearish is the contrary sentiment, meaning that a bearish investor or bear will think prices are falling.

These investor sentiments are not always based on fundamental analysis. Instead, they are driven by human emotion. Day traders and other financial analysts will use the market sentiment because short-term price movements are often influenced by investor attitudes towards particular financial security or industry. Contrarian investors also use market sentiment in order to trade in the opposing direction of the market. These attitudes can cause securities to be over- or undervalued in the market. This is why there are indicators used to measure market sentiment to gather more quantitative data. However, the majority of sentimental trading is based on the overall consensus of investors towards the market.

Pattern Trading

This style of trading involves using price patterns which are price movements that are tracked using curves and trendlines. This allows investors to recognize falling and rising trends in the market, which helps influence their trades. These patterns are noticeable formations created by connecting different price points such as opening and closing prices with a line on a graph. By using these formations, technical and financial analysts identify patterns to anticipate the future price movements of securities.

Trendlines are lines connecting the various highs and lows of price points during a time period. If a trendline is curved upwards, referred to as an up trendline, this means prices of a security are experiencing new higher peaks and new higher troughs or lows. In contrast, a down trendline signifies prices are experiencing lower troughs and lower highs. Trendlines with more than two price points are generally more sustainable and better for making informed investment decisions.

Swing Trading

Swing trading attempts to capture short to medium-term gains in securities for a profit over the span of days or weeks. Swing traders will use fundamental and technical analysis in conjunction with price trends and patterns for finding investment opportunities. The goal of this strategy is to catch capital gain on price movements by identifying an asset's next move, entering a position, and then profiting if that price change happens. The most popular financial security to trade in swing trading is large-cap stocks. Stocks swing between broad defined highs and lows over the course of days and weeks. Swing investors will follow these waves and reverse when the stocks do, keeping up with the value.

This form of trading is one of the most popular for short to medium-term opportunities. Some swing investors will choose volatile stocks with lots of movement to speed up the daily process. At the same time, others go for more sedated stocks which might take longer to profit from but also limits risk. Both these investors, however, are open to running the risk of opening a session after a night or a weekend to substantially different prices. Abrupt market fluctuations such as one-time news announcements can also result in substantial losses. Due to the short-term nature of swing trading, these investors often miss out on longer-term trends and opportunities in favor of quicker financial gain.

The major difference between swing trading and day trading is the length of time involved. Day traders will close out their position at the end of the day when the market closes. However, swing traders will often hold onto securities overnight, risking gaps up and down against the last closing price. Because of this risk, swing traders often trade in smaller portions compared to day traders.

Chapter 3: Investment of Shares

Shares are units of financial assets or equity ownership in a corporation owned by investors who exchanged capital for them. There are two types of shares: common and preferred shares. Common shares offer investors corporate voting rights and profits through dividends and share price appreciation. Preferred shares, on the other hand, do not appreciate at a price. However, they do offer regular dividends and can be redeemed at an attractive price. Despite most companies having shares, only shares of public corporations can be found through the stock exchange. These corporations offer shares in exchange for financial capital that they use to operate and grow the company. More financial capital means bigger profits, leading to more shares being issued in hopes of more capital. This is an investment cycle that keeps economic markets running.

Stop-Loss Orders

Stop-loss orders are like insurance policies set in place by investors to minimize losses on their investments, as their name suggests. These orders are automated and will buy or sell securities when a certain price is reached, all of which are based on the investor's criteria. For example, a trader can implement a stop-loss order for 20% below the price the security was initially bought at. This way, if a share that was originally bought at $30 and later on drops to $24, the order in place will automatically sell the share to prevent any more financial loss to the investor. These orders are popular in swing trading to limit multiple losses over multiple shares.

These fail-safes do not require constant supervision from the trader and minimize the losses for investors. They cost nothing to implement and remove human emotion and market sentiment from influencing trades that could be unprofitable. Holding onto a favored stock and blindly hoping for an uptrend does not make a smart investor.

However, these orders are not without fault. Since they are automated and happen instantly, a short-term fluctuation in the market can cause the order to sell shares that could cause a potential uptrend in the near future. Since some shares are known to fluctuate easier than others, a slight movement in price can end in the loss of potential profitable investments. Keep in mind that there are no recommended percentages for stop-loss orders as it all depends on the individual investor. A short-term investor may set lower percentages to limit their losses on multiple fluctuating shares. In contrast, a long-term trader will set higher percentages since they understand the market fluctuations and are gaining profits through dividends and other resources. No matter the kind of investor, anyone can benefit from implementing stop-loss orders in their trading strategy.

Technical Analysis

Technical analysis is considered a trading discipline, which is used to identify trading opportunities seen through price trends and market patterns. Technical analysts will gather historical data on statistical trends gathered from previous trading activity, such as price movement and volume. This qualitative data of the market helps investors make educated assumptions about their financial securities and current investments.

Technical analysis tools are used to study the ways supply and demand for financial securities will affect changes in volume, price, and implied volatility. These tools often help generate short-term charts and patterns that can provide investors with insight into the state of various assets in the market. Since almost all tradable instruments are subject to the forces of supply and demand, price movements of stocks, bonds, etc. can be predicted with technical analysis.

There are three base market assumptions that technical analysts will make. First is the theory that the market discounts everything. This means that a company's economic fundamentals and broader market factors like market sentiment are already priced into securities. Therefore the only thing left is the analysis of price movements, which is shown through the market's supply and demand. Second, the price of securities, regardless of the time frame observed, will always follow a trend despite the random nature of the market. Meaning the price of a stock is more likely to follow a previous trend than it is to move erratically. Finally, technical analysts believe that history will inevitably repeat itself which explains the repetitive nature of price movements that are affected by market psychology. Human emotions like fear and excitement will affect market sentiment, which then affects the price of securities within their downtrend window or uptrend window.

Fundamental Analysis

Fundamental analysis is the method of measuring an asset's intrinsic value or its worth by examining the related financial and economic factors. Anything that can affect an asset's worth is analyzed and taken into consideration. Microeconomic factors like a company's internal management, macroeconomic factors including industry conditions and the market as a whole are all analyzed. All this data is examined in hopes to give the fundamental analyst a fair market value that will help determine if an asset is over or undervalued when compared to its current market price. These values are estimations to determine if an asset will either appreciate or depreciate in the near future. If an asset is deemed to be undervalued by a fundamental analyst, then that means that its current value should rise in the future to match its fair market value.

Quantitative values like income statements and balance sheets are not the only fundamental factors that come into play when determining a fair market value or, as some investors call it, the company's intrinsic value. Qualitative factors such as a company's business model, their customer base, and their local and global competition can affect an asset's intrinsic value. Market share is a popular qualitative value that represents the percentage of total sales within an economic industry generated by a specific corporation. If a company's market share is growing, that means that it is generating more revenues than its competitors. Increased market share allows for higher profitability and greater operations and business investments. Companies grow their market share by lowering prices and advertising to increase their consumer base or introducing new products and services to generate demands and revenues. This tool is used to show a company's financial market power in relations to their competitors.

As mentioned before, both technical and fundamental analysis are two major schools of thought when it comes to who views the market. The core of the technical analysis is that all known fundamentals are already factored into the price of securities meaning they hold little to no importance. Fundamentalists evaluate their securities by measuring their intrinsic value. At the same time, technical investors will instead use charts to identify patterns and trends that will predict the future price movements of financial assets.

Portfolio Diversification

Portfolio diversification is an investment strategy that attempts to limit investors' potential financial risks by having varying assets in their portfolios. This allows for their securities with positive performances to help cushion the blow of investments that are performing negatively. This works best with securities that are not correlated, or that do not belong to the same sector, as this strategy requires opposing investments that guarantee that when one asset is down another will go up.

Portfolio diversification is simple. Instead of investing all their capital into one asset class such as stocks, investors will spread out their capital into multiple investment classes, including stocks, bonds, real estate, etc. Then within each asset class, there are other means of varying a portfolio such as investing in different sectors, various market capitalizations, even investing abroad into foreign securities that are less correlated to at home market fluctuations.

Diversifying one's portfolio is very important in order to mitigate risk and potential losses while acting as a buffer for market volatility. However, this strategy also comes with its share of disadvantages. For instance, the increased amount of holding required to diversify a portfolio can increase fees relating to transactions, trading, and broker commission. It is also more time-consuming to manage a portfolio, which could mean needing to hire a portfolio manager, which is another expense. Therefore this spreading-out strategy of portfolio diversification works both ways by lessening both the reward and the risk of portfolio investments.

Chapter 4: Investing in Options and Bonds

What Are Options?

A stock option is like an investor's right to buy or sell a stock at an agreed-upon price and time; however, these are no obligations. Two types of stock options exist: a call and a put. The former is a bet that a stock's price will fall, while the latter is a bet that a stock's price will rise. Beyond the two types, there are also two styles of stock options: American and European. American options can be used anytime between the purchase and the expiration date, while European options can only be used on the expiration date and are less common than their American counterpart.

As in any form of investment, short-term and long-term stock options exist. Short-term options usually have a range of days or weeks between purchase and their expiration date. These types of options are often cheaper in price because of their low time value. They are usually placed before a major event such as a company conference, economic reports, or bigger national events like a presidential election. The nature of the event can have major effects on these options, with the value either greatly increasing afterward or decreasing to nothing. Long-term options, on the other hand, have an expiration date that is six months or more away from the purchase date. They are more expensive than their short-term counterparts. However, they require less financial capital than buying stocks in bulk allowing investors to gain leverage in a stock. Since these underlying stocks will start to use value if the stock starts to decrease, they do require appreciation in order for them to be profitable. Because their value stagnates or decreases, it is an automatic loss.

An options contract is used as the agreement between two parties to exchange capital and securities at a preset day and price. Investors must pay a premium for the rights that the contract grants. For stock options, the contract represents 100 shares of the underlying stock. Therefore, call options are leveraged bets on the appreciation of financial security, while put options are the same for depreciating stock prices.

Both options can be profitable for their respective investors. Call option buyers are assuming that the share price will rise above the purchased or strike price before the option's expiration date. If this happens, the bullish investor can use their option to buy the stocks at the strike price and immediately be able to sell them at their current price for a profit. On the other hand, call option sellers are bearish in nature since they assume the value of their shares will remain constant or depreciate. The maximum profitable income the seller of the call option will receive is the premium paid for the option. However, the seller can lose money if the value instead appreciates, as now the seller must fulfill the option by either selling their own shares or buying shares at current market value and selling those.

Put option buyers want stock prices to decrease. This is because if the market price were to drop below the strike price at expiry, the investor could utilize their put option which is to sell the shares at the option's higher price point. The profit in this scenario is the strike price minus the current market value plus expenses, which includes premiums and commissions. This result is then multiplied by the number of option contracts purchased, then again by 100, with the assumption that each contract is 100 stocks. The risk associated with buying put options is limited to the loss of the premium if the options were to expire worthlessly.

Sellers of put options are bullish writers of options contracts, meaning their maximum profit is the premium charged if the stock price closes above the strike price. However, if the value of the stocks drops below the strike price, the writer must buy the shares at the strike price, meaning the option was exercised by the buyer. The buyer sells their shares at the strike price since their value has surpassed the stock market price. Depending on how far the value has depreciated, the put seller's loss can be significant despite any cushioning the premium may provide.

What Are Bonds?

Bonds are instruments representing a loan from an investor to a borrower, who are usually corporations or organizations. They are referred to as fixed-income instruments. This is due to being traditionally paid a fixed interest rate to debtholders, however, floating or variable interest rates are now common. A bond is a sort of IOU between the lender and borrower that describes the details of the loan and its repayments. Those details also include the end date of the repayments along with either the fixed or variable interest rates. Because of this, bond rates are correlated to each other; when those rates increase, the price of the bonds decreases and vice-versa.

Corporations and governments use bonds to finance their operations and projects, while owners of these bonds are creditors or debtholders to the issuers. These loans do have expiration dates in which the principal amount needs to be paid entirely or risk default. Since both organizations often need to borrow more money than banks can provide, bonds act as a way for multiple investors to act as lenders. Hundreds to thousands of investors can all lend a portion of the borrowing amount through public debt markets. Also, through these markets, investors can also buy and sell bonds with each other even after the initial organization received their capital.

Most bonds initial pricing is usually set at par, meaning at $100 or $1,000 denominations per bond. Factors such as the credit quality of the issuer and the maturity of the loan determine the market value of bonds. Through trading bonds, investors can repurchase bonds that receive changes in either their interest rates or the issuer's credit quality.

Here are some terms that are commonly used to discuss bonds. First, there is "face value," which refers to the amount that the bond will be worth at the end of its maturity date. This amount is also used to calculate interest rate payments. Another term is coupon rate, which is the rate usually expressed as a percentage of the interest the bond issuer will pay on the face value of the bond. For example, a coupon rate of 7% for a bond of $1,000 face value means the bondholders will receive $70 per coupon date, which refers to the date that interest payments are made. These payments can be paid at any interval but semiannually is the most common.

Government and Agency Bonds

Government bonds, or treasury securities, are divided into three different categories based on their maturity and are one of the safest investments in the market. The first category is T-Bills which have the shortest maturity of the three government bonds. These bonds are issued at varying times, usually in only a matter of days, with a maximum maturity of 52 weeks. Commonly sold in denominations of $1,000, the interest rates for T-Bills depend on the length of maturity. Since these are government-issued securities, they are considered a conservative and safe investment. They can also be sold before the maturity date to another investor for a short-term gain depending on their value on the market.

The second category of treasury securities are T-Notes, which have maturity dates ranging from two to ten years. T-Notes' interest rates are fixed and depend on the length of their maturity, and their payments occur semiannually. In contrast to T-Bills, these securities are issued at par of $100, and the treasury auctions the medium-range bonds starting from one year to seven-year T-Notes on a monthly basis. At the same time, longer ten-year long-maturity bonds are auctioned on specific months through the year, often quarterly. The third category of T-Bonds follows the same guidelines as T-Notes; however, the main difference is their lengths as T-Bonds can have maturity terms of 30 years.

The main benefit of Treasury securities is that they are backed by the full faith and credit of the government. Therefore investors are guaranteed their return via both interest rates and the principal amount of the bond, as long as they are held until maturity. These bonds are also tax-exempt at the local and municipal levels. However, since these bonds are taxable at the federal level, any gains and losses need to be declared every tax season.

While Government Bonds are issued by a treasury, agency bonds are issued directly from a government department or a government-sponsored corporation. These bonds are completely backed by the government, meaning that interest rates and face value returns are guaranteed. They are often sold in increments of $10,000 and offer slightly greater interest rates than Treasury securities. The main risk for either bond is their interest rates. An investor buying such bonds in 2017 might have lower interest rates than an investor buying the same bond in 2020 and vice versa. Due to their long position nature, these bonds should match the individual investors' financial needs and wants.

Corporate Bonds

As aforementioned, corporate bonds are issued when a corporation needs capital to finance future business endeavors, and they can be bought through an equity firm, brokers, or directly on the market through online platforms. These bonds work like an IOU, with the business promising to repay the face value of the bond by a preset date along with the regular interest rate payments throughout the year. All corporate bonds come with a bond rating which aims to calculate the risk associated with each bond issue. These ratings are based on many factors such as growth potential, financial stability, and any current corporate debt. Such factors help assign letter grades to bonds which helps investors know whether or not the issuer can repay their debt or might default on their obligation. Bond ratings that are AAA to BBB are considered good investment grades, meaning they are often safer and more stable investments with low potential risk. Anything lower than a BBB is considered a junk bond. A junk bond suggests a company with liquidity problems with potentially a higher investment risk, however, maybe bigger yields.

Since the market is ever-changing, longer bonds typically have higher interest rates in order to entice investors to agree to higher bond prices in return for more profit. Some bonds are called redeemable bonds, and these can be redeemed anytime before the maturity date. Despite the investor losing out on the continuation of the interest rate payments, the corporation does pay a premium.

Although no corporate bonds are completely risk-free due to the fluctuating market, these bonds do offer a steady income due to their interest rates over the lifetime of the bond. For financial insurance, if a business were to declare bankruptcy during the lifetime of their bonds, bondholders do have a claim on their cash and assets. These bonds help diversify portfolios and allow for a slightly more stable investment option.

Municipal Bonds

Just like with many bonds, municipal bonds refer to investors lending money to receive interest rates over the course of the bond along with the face value amount loaned at the maturity date. These bonds come both in taxable and tax-exempt formats, with the latter being the most favored. Investors seeking a tax-free income source while holding onto capital will flock to tax-exempt municipal bonds. These bonds are separated into two varieties: general obligation bonds, which are used to raise immediate funds, and revenue bonds, which are used to finance infrastructure projects. Both of these are considered low risk since issuers are almost guaranteed to honor their bonds and pay back debt.

As with the bonds previously discussed here, there are many strategies when it comes to buying and exchanging bonds in order to make capital gains. The most simple of them is to buy bonds with enticing interest rates and hold them to their maturity. This way, the investor has a steady stream of income via interest rates along with their return. Even if the bond is paid out, a premium is issued to the bondholder as a reward for the early debt retirement. Another, more complex strategy is the creation of something called a "municipal bond ladder." These ladders are a series of bonds with varying interest rates and maturity dates. When one bond matures, the original capital from the bond is reinvested into another bond, continuing the steady income. These forms of investment are considered passive due to the fact that the bonds are held until maturity and do not require much oversight. An active investor might buy bonds and sell them instead to generate profits from selling them at a premium on the market. Despite municipal bonds not being as risk-free as government bonds, they act as tax-havens that offer greater returns than their government counterparts.

Chapter 5: Mutual Funds and Precious Metals

Mutual Funds are portfolios consisting of stocks, bonds, and other securities that give investors access to portfolios that are already diversified professionally. They usually charge annual fees as well as any commissions or premiums for the money manager in charge. These mutual funds are categorized by the sectors that they represent or the combination of securities they hold. An example of such would be the majority of employer-sponsored retirement plans set by corporations.

Investors' money gets pooled into these mutual funds, which are later used to buy other securities like stocks or bonds. These investments will influence the value of the mutual fund. When an investor partakes in mutual funds, they are not investing in individual securities. Instead, they are investing in the value of the portfolio as a whole. Therefore, holders of mutual funds do not acquire any individual stock benefits such as voting rights. The price of a mutual fund is referred to as Net Asset Value per share, shortened to NAV or NAVPS. The NAV is influenced by the value of the securities that create the mutual fund. These NAVs do not fluctuate during day trading hours. Instead, they are settled at the end of market hours meaning that the value of the mutual fund is determined when the NAV is settled.

Investors' income through mutual funds is gained as annual distributions of dividends from the portfolio's stocks and bond investments. This capital can either be taken as profit or reinvested into the mutual fund. Also included in the distribution are any profits gained from selling portfolio securities. Investors can also sell their mutual funds for a profit if the NAV is higher than when they originally bought.

A mutual fund can be seen as a virtual company, with fund managers who are also usually the owners, legally forced to work in the best interest of mutual fund shareholders.

Exchange Traded Funds

An exchange traded fund, or ETF for short, is a type of security that tracks a sector, index or other asset that can then be purchased or sold on a stock exchange like a regular stock. Think of it like a basket of securities that investors can trade on an exchange, just like a regular stock. ETFs have the possibility to contain various types of investments such as financial commodities, stocks or bonds while offering lower expense ratios and commissions in comparison to buying individual stocks to trade on the market. Comparable to mutual funds, these ETFs have their prices updated throughout the day as they are bought and sold. Mutual funds instead are not traded on an exchange and only after the market is closed. Therefore exchange traded funds are considered more liquid and cost-effective than mutual funds.

There are various types of ETFs, such as Bond ETFs, which can include the government and corporate bonds aforementioned in this book. Industry ETFs track specific industries such as oil, technology and banking while currency ETFs participate in the investment of foreign currencies.

The advantages of investing into exchange traded funds are that they provide investors with lower expenses. ETFs are cheaper than buying all the individual stocks and broker commissions and transaction fees are also lessened with ETFs in comparison. Some brokers even offer no to low commissions on low-cost ETFs which helps reduce investor expenses even more. ETFs also offer access to a larger variety of holdings across sectors and industries which in turn help diversify an investment portfolio, minimizing long-term losses.

While most ETFs are considered a passive investment, there are actively-managed ETFs which involve portfolio managers buying, selling and changing the holdings within the fund. These funds are usually more costly, but they offer greater market oversight. Other disadvantages of investing into ETFs can include their lack of liquidity, which hinders their market transactions. Also, ETFs that focus on one sector or industry remove their diversification nature in financial portfolios.

Income Funds

Income funds are mutual funds or exchange-traded funds that prioritize current income instead of appreciation of values and capital gains. These funds are low-risk and often are made up of bonds, other fixed-income securities, and dividends. Just as with mutual portfolios, the share prices of these income funds are not fixed, meaning that they will fall when the market interest rates increase and vice versa. Typically these portfolios only contain investment-grade bonds, in addition to securities with sufficient credit, quality to ensure the preservation of capital.

Income Funds come in various types, depending on the types of securities invested into. Bond-Funds are normally investments of government or corporation bonds. Government bonds, as previously mentioned, are virtually low risk, which makes good investment options during a time of market uncertainty. Corporations, on the other hand, carry a slight chance that they cannot make interest payments or that they will default on the bond. Due to this risk, they often pay higher interest rates to entice investors. These bonds are classified as investment-grade or junk bonds, depending on their bond rating.

When funds are invested predominantly into stocks that have regular dividend payouts, they become known as equity income funds. These funds offer investors regular stable income via dividends generated by their portfolios. Equity income funds are a popular investment for retirees as it provides predictable profits on a monthly basis.

Index Funds

Index Funds are a kind of mutual fund or ETF that are constructed to track the components of a financial market index, which are hypothetical portfolios of investment holdings that represent a piece of the actual financial market. The value of these indexes comes from their underlying holdings, and investors use "weighting" to adjust and understand the individual impact of items in an index. Revenue-weighted and fundamental-weighting are typical examples of adjusted individual values in indexes.

Returning to index funds, these portfolios of stocks are designed to imitate the behavior and performance of a financial market index. These provide investors with low operations fees and portfolio turnover as well as broader exposure to the market as they hold various securities. A fund manager will create an index mutual fund containing holding that matches the securities of a certain index. The assumption is that if that index is faring well, so will the holdings in a similar sector. Because of this and the long-term commitment of mutual index funds, they are considered passive investments. However, they are also considered core financial portfolio investments for individual retirement accounts.

Actively managed mutual funds are usually more expensive than their passive counterparts due to their increased number of staff and market transactions. These fees can mean losses that, in the long run, compare to a passive mutual fund. However, in the short term, these actively run funds can generate greater profits. The overall low fees for mutual index funds is why they have become a popular long-term investment option for the passive investor.

Precious Metals

Precious metals are highly valuable metals because of their uses in industrial businesses and their historical role as stores of value.

Their scarcity also increases their value, making precious metals rare and valuable economic instruments. The most common precious metals for investors include silver, gold, and platinum. Specifically, gold and silver, when at least 99.5% pure, are called Bullion. Investors mainly invest in these metals as financial assets, but they also help diversify portfolios.

There are various ways to acquire stock in precious metals. One way is to purchase physical stock such as minted bars and coins; however, this incurs storage and insurance fees as well as the risk of theft. Another way is to buy future contracts of the precious metal or acquire shares in a corporation that deals in precious metals exploration and production. One can also use mutual funds to include securities in mining and such.

The Bullion market is like the stock market but for precious metals. It is where gold and silver along with other precious metals are sold, bought and traded. The London Bullion Market is the primary market of its kind, operating 24 hours a day and overseeing the futures and options trading. The few corporations with a membership to the London Bullion Market exchange gain the majority of their revenues from gold and silver. A good portion of Bullion is held in reserve in central banks, making up approximately 20% of all mined gold.

Types of Precious Metals

Gold is valued 24 hours a day, seven days a week, and is mostly unaffected by supply and demand. Instead, the price of gold is influenced by market sentiment. This is because the current hoarded supply of gold greatly outweighs the mining supply. Therefore, gold hoarders can drive the price down by supplying the market with more gold. Any new supply of gold is quickly absorbed by investors and gold hoarders alike, driving the price up. Gold hoarders include central banks that use precious metals for their many financial benefits.

Silver, like gold, is often hoarded as a store of value; however, its value changes due to its importance as an industrial metal. Because of this, the supply and demand of production industries for silver exert a heavy influence on its price. This means that the value of silver is more volatile than gold, increasing when industry demands are high while decreasing when not. Examples of this are the decrease in silver's value in the photography industry with the invention of digital cameras to the rise of silver in batteries, micro conduits markets, and technological industries.

Another precious metal traded is platinum, which is more valuable than gold because it is a rarer natural resource. Other than its rarity, additional factors determine its value. Like silver, platinum has many different industrial uses, from automobiles and jewelry to computers. Russia and South Africa have the biggest concentrations of platinum mines, and this creates issues on a global scale, such as cartel wars and market trust, that can drive prices. The automobile industry also relies heavily on platinum which drives prices up as cleaner cars are made. However, palladium, which is platinum's less expensive sister metal, could replace it, causing uncertainty for platinum's value. All these factors make this metal the most volatile out of the three.

Investing in the precious metal carries no credit risk or fear of inflation while also offering investors some form of financial insurance during political or global crises. They also help decrease the volatility and risks when incorporated in portfolios, acting as a sort of safety blanket. Through investing in mutual funds, acquiring Bullion of precious metals, and purchasing contract futures, investors can soften financial blows and gain financial security. As the value of securities fluctuates on a rapid basis, precious metals offer investors a stable store of values.

Chapter 6: Real Estate Investments

Investing in real estate can be a profitable investment; however, being a landlord requires a lot of initial capital and can come with many expenses. Landlord expenses include mortgage and property taxes, and the job itself requires one to maintain their estates, find tenants and deal with inconveniences. Being a landlord is a hands-on investment unless a property manager is hired, which is another expense of real estate investments. Choosing neighborhoods, tenants, and employees carefully will help minimize risks.

Despite the amount of work required, becoming a landlord is a profitable investment. The first form of profit is charging rent to tenants, which is determined by the value of the property and location. Charge too much rent and you will limit the number of possible tenants; charge too little and you won't maximize your profits. A rule of thumb is to charge enough to cover mortgage payments until they are paid off, at which point the majority of the rent becomes profits. Another way to generate revenues is through value appreciation. Real estate tends to appreciate in value, meaning that it can be sold at a higher price point later on. Despite this, there are no guarantees that properties will appreciate as many factors come into play when determining neighborhood and property values.

While this style of investment is more passively long-term, there are house flippers of real estate, just like the day traders of the stock market. House flippers purchase real estate for short periods of time and then resell at a higher price. How so? These real estate investors can purchase properties and then repair and update them quickly to resell them new and improved. In doing so, one has to ensure that the value will increase with these upgrades and ensure that the new price covers the capital invested enough to be profitable. Another way to profit off real estate rapidly is to buy property in a rising market and then resell it at its new valued price after a few months.

With either type of house flipping, the investor must make sure that the revenue generated will cover the costs enough to be financially beneficial. Poor construction engineering can delay repairs and increase long-term expenses. A market could not rise as much as presumed, leaving a landlord to now choose between renting the property and reselling it at a limited price.

Real Estate Groups

Real Estate Investment Trust

Real Estate Investment Trusts are companies that own, finance, and operate revenue-generating real estate properties. They invest in most real estate types such as hotels, apartments, warehouses, and more. Modeled after mutual funds, they pool the capital of many investors, allowing investors to earn dividends from their investments without needing to own, manage or finance their own properties. Most real estate investment trusts, or REITs, are publicly traded like stocks. This offers them increased liquidity compared to physical real estate. These trusts give investors a steady income via dividends; however, they have little to no means of capital appreciation.

There are three types of REITs, with the most common one being equity REITs. These are managed and owned properties that generate the majority of their income through rent and not through reselling. Then, there are mortgage real estate investment trusts that lend money to owners and operators of real estate. This capital can be borrowed directly through loans and mortgages or through the acquiring of mortgage-backed securities. The net interest margin, which is the margin between the expense of funding these loans and the charged interest rates, is what generates revenues in mortgage REITs. This makes this type of investment particularly sensitive to fluctuations in interest rates. The final type is hybrid REITs which are a combination of both aforementioned types.

Investors use both equity and mortgage strategies to generate income.

Depending on how these investments are bought and held, they can also be classified as publicly, non-publicly, or privately traded stock. Publicly traded REITs have shares that are tradable on the stock exchange, which are then bought by individual investors. These shares are regulated by governments' financial departments. As its name states, non-publicly traded REITs are still on the stock market, but they are non-tradable on national stock exchanges. Because of this, they are less liquid than their traded counterparts, but they are less susceptible to changes in the market. Private REITs, on the other hand, are not traded at all on national securities exchanges and can only be bought by institutional investors.

REITs are great additions to investment portfolios because they offer investors long-term income through dividends and diversification of securities. Since most people trade on the stock exchange, they are easy to buy and sell, which their traditional brick and mortar counterparts lack. Their liquidity, along with their attractive risk-adjusted returns, is enticing to many investors. However, they have a low potential for capital appreciation due to most of the revenue going back to investors as income instead of reinvesting in new holdings. They are also subject to market changes in addition to high management fees, transactions, and dividends being taxable income may sway investors to take their investment elsewhere.

Before moving on, real estate mutual funds must be discussed. These are mutual funds that typically will invest into real estate operations or REITs. These mutual funds offer investors a diversified exposure with a broader range of real estate investments for less financial capital than purchasing individual investment trusts. Like REITs, real estate mutual funds are pretty liquid, and they also offer analytical insight into certain real estate investments. Investing in a multitude of mutual funds with different outweighing assets and property types can give investors research information on real estate while maximizing returns.

Real Estate Investment Groups

Real Estate Investment Groups, or REIGs, are entities that focus the majority of the business investments into real estate. To generate profits, these groups will either buy, renovate, sell or invest in properties. Commonly they will purchase a property and rent units to other investors while staying in charge of administration and maintenance. These real estate investment groups also usually do not qualify for REIT status, meaning they are not held down by real estate regulations and requirements.

REITs are made up of multiple partners and shareholders who pool together their financial capital in order to make greater and broader investments. Since only the majority of their business needs to be in real estate, they have flexibility in their internally structured and make investments as desired. REITs will often lease properties to real estate management companies or clients in exchange for a portion of the rent. They can also sell units of the property but still maintain overall control. Since there are no true limitations on REIGs' business activities, they are often marketed as real estate investment groups to attract investors.

The structure of these groups is commonly a partnership or a corporation. The former is a partnership of two or more investors who share profits, losses, and expenses, and their stakes are usually proportional to their investments. Depending on the structure of the partnership, some are more collaborative, while others have members who do not participate in the daily business aspects. However, these partners still receive their profits, voting rights, and other partnership perks outlined in their contracts. The latter, on the other hand, is the formation of either a public or private corporation. Incorporating a business allows its shares to be traded for equity which helps fund operations and reinvestments. Because of this, however, they are regulated by financial departments, and public equity is subject to value fluctuation along with the market while private equity is valued privately. Online real estate platforms now allow for crowdfunding which allows for accredited and non-accredited investors to pool capital for investments. These follow the same structure as partnerships.

Similarly, real estate limited partnerships, or RELPs, are similar to real estate investment groups because they both are entities that buy and hold a property or portfolios of properties. These partnerships, however, only last a limited amount of years. The general partner is usually a real estate development firm or a property manager. Whoever it is, they seek out financial capital from other investors who then become limited partners. During the partnership, the partners all receive the periodic income generated through the RELPs properties. However, the biggest gain is from the selling of actual properties followed by the partnership dissolving in the future.

Why Invest in Real Estate

Generally speaking, the real estate market has low volatility, especially when compared to other securities like bonds and equities. It also has somewhat of a negative correlation with other financial assets. In most cases, when stock values are low, real estate is high. This allows for portfolio diversification and protection against the risks of other securities. More direct real estate investments allow for a better hedge, which means using multiple financial securities to offset price changes and minimize risk. Less direct investments such as REITs or real estate mutual funds are always going to reflect the market and therefore offer less in terms of portfolio hedging.

However, all real estate investments have an inflation hedging capability. This is due to the positive relationship real estate has with a country's GDP, or Gross Domestic Product. The expansion of economies increases the demand for real estate, which drives up prices and, in turn, means higher capital. Thus, real estate maintains purchasing power of capital and redistributes inflation onto tenants, and incorporates some through capital appreciation.

One investment tool only found in real estate, with the exception of REITs, is leverage. When buying stocks, one must pay the full value of the stock at the time of purchase. However, with mortgages, investors can have multiple real estate investments that are not all paid for. Most mortgages ask for a 20% down payment; however, those down payments can be as low as 5%. Despite not paying for the property in full, the investor owns and has full control of it as soon as the papers are signed. This entices house flippers and landlords because they use mortgages and acquire multiple properties without having the total valued capital. With full control of these assets, investors can rent out units, hold to resell, and renovate to increase the value, which all contribute to profits in the long run despite only having paid a portion of the total value.

As with any investments, real estate does have its downsides. Since it is hard to convert immediately into cash, it is considered illiquid, with real estate transactions taking up to multiple months to complete. While REITs and real estate mutual funds do offer better liquidity and follow the value of the market, they are more volatile. They also offer less portfolio diversification since they are more correlated to the market compared to direct real estate investments.

Whether directly investing, taking on the duties of a landlord, or participating in real estate groups, real estate can be a profitable investment. This is a financial investment with the potential to provide investors with a regular steady income. With realistic expectations of the labor involved and tons of prior research, real estate investors can greatly increase their personal wealth.

Conclusion

Investing can be scary, but it should not be. Historically, it seemed as if only those with established financial ties could participate in the market. The abundance of economic terms, confusing graphs, and lack of access to investment knowledge can push potential investors away. All the numbers, market variables, fluctuations, and risks associated with it make it seem like a concept only knowledgeable people can participate in. However, if you are reading this part of the book, you know that anyone and everyone can invest. No matter the age, experience or financial capital of the trader.

Now it is time to do some personal exploration and reflection. Are you an active day-trader who can weather the potential risks for an even bigger reward? Or are you a buy-and-hold type of investor with future goals that these investments will benefit from? Do you know what sector to invest in, or would you rather hire someone to build you a professional financial portfolio and increase your chance of success? All these questions need to be answered in order to create the perfect investment strategy that is molded to your personal goals and desires. Finding out what investments works for you and which ones do not is part of the process.

Now, you have the instruments necessary to take that first leap in the world of investments. You can now incorporate short and long-term investments in your financial portfolio to boost your economic standing. You know how to save, invest and grow your wealth through not only the stock market but also through precious metals, real estate, and mutual funds. This book has given you a foundation of investment knowledge, and now you can be a more comfortable investor.

So does one need to be a financial expert to trade and invest? Absolutely not.

If you enjoyed this book in anyway, an honest
review is always appreciated!

References

Anderson, A. (2019). Investing: Invest Like A Pro: Stocks, ETFs, Options, Mutual Funds, Precious Metals and Bonds. Lulu.com.

Chen, J. (2019). Primary Market. Investopedia. https://www.investopedia.com/terms/p/primarymarket.asp

Chen, J. (2020, December 31). Contrarian Definition. Investopedia. https://www.investopedia.com/terms/c/contrarian.asp

Cussen, M. P. (2019, March 19). Introduction to Treasury Securities. Investopedia. https://www.investopedia.com/articles/investing/073113/introduction-treasury-securities.asp

Frey, A. H. (2013). A beginner's guide to investing : how to grow your money the smart and easy way. Ivy Bytes.

Investopedia. (2010). Bond Basics Tutorial. http://i.investopedia.com/inv/pdf/tutorials/bondbasics.pdf

Investopedia. (2020a, August 31). A Real Estate Investing Guide. Investopedia. https://www.investopedia.com/mortgage/real-estate-investing-guide/

Investopedia. (2020b, September 5). Active vs. Passive Investing: What's Best for You? Investopedia. https://www.investopedia.com/news/active-vs-passive-investing/

Kenton, W. (2019). Secondary Market. Investopedia. https://www.investopedia.com/terms/s/secondarymarket.asp

Kramer, M. (2020, July 1). Over-The-Counter Market Definition.
 Investopedia.
 https://www.investopedia.com/terms/o/over-the-
 countermarket.asp

Langager, C. (2019). A Beginner's Guide to Stock Investing.
 Investopedia.
 https://www.investopedia.com/articles/basics/06/invest10
 00.asp

Laopodis, N. T. (2020). Understanding Investments: Theories and
 Strategies (2nd ed.). Routledge.
 https://doi.org/10.4324/9781003027478

SEC, & UNITED STATES - SECURITIES AND EXCHANGE
 COMMISSION. (2010). Mutual Funds A Guide for Investors
 Information is an investor's best tool.
 https://www.sec.gov/investor/pubs/sec-guide-to-
 mutual-funds.pdf

U.S. Securities and Exchange Commission. (n.d.). Saving and
 Investing for Students. Retrieved April 23, 2021, from
 https://www.sec.gov/investor/pubs/savings-investing-
 for-students.pdf

Young Investors Society. (2016). Stock investing 101. Yis.org; Young
 Investors Society. https://yis.org/wp-
 content/uploads/2016/10/Stock-Investing-101-eBook.pdf

www.ingramcontent.com/pod-product-compliance
Lightning Source LLC
Chambersburg PA
CBHW031910200326
41597CB00012B/574